W9-CBF-719

THE EVOLUTION OF
Reptiles

by Sue Bradford Edwards

Content Consultant

Peter Uetz
Associate Professor
Center for the Study of Biological Complexity
Virginia Commonwealth University

Essential Library

An Imprint of Abdo Publishing | abdobooks.com

ANIMAL EVOLUTION

abdobooks.com

Published by Abdo Publishing, a division of ABDO, PO Box 398166, Minneapolis, Minnesota 55439. Copyright © 2019 by Abdo Consulting Group, Inc. International copyrights reserved in all countries. No part of this book may be reproduced in any form without written permission from the publisher. Essential Library™ is a trademark and logo of Abdo Publishing.

Printed in the United States of America, North Mankato, Minnesota.
092018
012019

THIS BOOK CONTAINS
RECYCLED MATERIALS

Cover Photo: iStockphoto
Interior Photos: Mohamed Abd El Ghany/Reuters/Newscom, 4–5; Laurie O'Keefe/Science Source, 7, 48; Christian Darkin/Science Source, 9; The Natural History Museum, London/Science Source, 13; Shutterstock Images, 15 (diagram), 15 (tortoise), 28–29, 50–51, 64, 76, 80–81; Kuttelvaserova Stuchelova/Shutterstock Images, 17; iStockphoto, 18–19, 38, 69; Frans Lanting/MINT Images/Science Source, 21; B. G. Thomson/Science Source, 22; Thierry Berrod, Mona Lisa Production/Science Source, 24–25; Mark Moffett/Minden Pictures/Newscom, 27; Daniel Naupold/picture-alliance/dpa/AP Images, 32; National News/ZumaPress/Newscom, 35; Michael Smith ITWP/Shutterstock Images, 36; Steve Byland/Shutterstock Images, 37; Jay Ondreicka/Shutterstock Images, 39; Meister Photos/Shutterstock Images, 40–41; Michel Gunther/Science Source, 43; Millard H. Sharp/Science Source, 45, 52; Franny Constantina/Shutterstock Images, 57; Tom Reichner/Shutterstock Images, 59; Kurit Afshen/Shutterstock Images, 60–61; Noah Poritz/Science Source, 62; Gudkov Andrey/Shutterstock Images, 70–71; AY Images/iStockphoto, 73; Jaime Chirinos/Science Source, 78–79; David Callan/iStockphoto, 83; Cathy Keifer/Shutterstock Images, 84; Svoboda Pavel/Shutterstock Images, 86; Jan Bures/Shutterstock Images, 89; Holly Guerrio/Shutterstock Images, 90–91; Xinhua/Sipa USA/Newscom, 95; James L. Amos/Science Source, 96

Editor: Marie Pearson
Series Designer: Becky Daum

Library of Congress Control Number: 2018947970

Publisher's Cataloging-in-Publication Data

Names: Edwards, Sue Bradford, author.
Title: The evolution of reptiles / by Sue Bradford Edwards.
Description: Minneapolis, Minnesota : Abdo Publishing, 2019 | Series: Animal evolution | Includes online resources and index.
Identifiers: ISBN 9781532116674 (lib. bdg.) | ISBN 9781532159510 (ebook)
Subjects: LCSH: Reptiles--Evolution--Juvenile literature. | Animal evolution--Juvenile literature. | Biological evolution--Juvenile literature. | Reptiles--Juvenile literature.
Classification: DDC 574.30--dc23

CONTENTS

CHAPTER ONE

The End of the Age of the Dinosaurs

Paleontologist Sanaa Al-Sayed works to preserve a fossil of *Mansourasaurus shahinae*.

Mansourasaurus shahinae walked slowly down the beach. On one side of the dinosaur, waves lapped the sand. On the other side, the coastal jungle stretched into the distance. The dinosaur pulled a mouthful of leaves from the trees, chewed, and swallowed.

The jungle provided the food *M. shahinae* needed to survive. The dinosaur moved among the trees and other plants, eating its fill. From time to time, it scanned the area. The jungle that provided food also hid possible predators. The bony plates along *M. shahinae's* back offered some protection, but the massive animal was not invulnerable.

It wasn't fully grown yet, but it already weighed as much as a modern male African elephant. It was between 26 and 33 feet (8 and 10 m) long.[1] In the distance, it could hear the heavy footsteps of other *M. shahinae* as the dinosaurs foraged for food.

SIGNIFICANT FIND

In 2013, Dr. Hesham Sallam, head of the Department of Geology at Mansoura University in Mansoura, Egypt, took his crew into the desert 470 miles (750 km) southwest of Cairo.[2] For five years, they had been searching for fossils. He told his team to spread out to cover as much ground as possible.

As they walked, his cell phone rang. He was one mile (2 km) from the searcher who was calling. "Doctor, there are a lot of bones. Come and see them," she said.[3] As soon as he spotted the first bone, he suspected they had made a historic discovery.

His team had found a partial dinosaur skeleton. By the time they were done excavating, they had located part of the skull, the lower jaw, vertebrae from the neck and back, ribs,

Sauropods' long necks helped them reach food.

most of the shoulder and upper front leg, part of a hind foot, and pieces of armor plating.

The skeleton, more complete than many fossils, was a sauropod: a long-necked herbivorous, or plant-eating, dinosaur. They eventually named this new reptile *Mansourasaurus shahinae.* It lived approximately 80 million years ago (MYA) during the end of the Cretaceous

MASS EXTINCTION

At the end of the Cretaceous, all of the nonavian dinosaurs went extinct. The avian dinosaurs continued to evolve into birds. The dinosaurs weren't the only reptiles to be hit hard by this extinction event. So were two groups of ocean predators: mosasaurs and plesiosaurs. Scientists don't agree on what caused this global extinction, but they do know that it was something that changed the environment, causing greenhouse gases to rise and temperatures around the world to heat up. Some scientists believe this was caused by an asteroid striking Earth and throwing dust and dirt into the air. Others believe debris was thrown into the air when volcanoes erupted. Whatever the cause, plants that needed a lot of sunlight died out. Animals that ate these plants also died, as did animals that preyed on them. This mass extinction meant that other plants and animals had the opportunity to fill those niches, leading to the evolution of many new species. This period is sometimes known as the End-Cretaceous Extinction or the Cretaceous-Paleogene Extinction because the extinctions came between the Cretaceous and Paleogene (66–23 MYA) periods.

period (145–66 MYA), just before the majority of dinosaurs became extinct. It was approximately the length of a school bus and weighed about as much as an African elephant. Scientists know that it wasn't fully grown because its leg bones had not fully fused, a process in which bones in a young animal grow together as the animal ages. Its discovery was vitally important because very few fossils from the Cretaceous have been found in Africa. It is difficult to find fossils in Africa because so much of the land is covered in vegetation. Sallam and his crew made their find in the desert, where the soil and rocks are visible. Because so few African fossils have been found, all discoveries like Sallam's are important. This one is key because it also refutes a theory about the isolation of African dinosaurs.

Three hundred MYA, Earth's landmasses formed a single supercontinent, Pangaea. During the Cretaceous, this supercontinent divided into Gondwana, which included Africa, and Laurasia, which included Europe. Because of this split, many scientists believed that by the late Cretaceous, dinosaurs in Africa were isolated from those in Europe. Yet *M. shahinae* more closely resembled its European relatives than it resembled the sauropods of southern Africa. Africa was not as isolated as scientists had thought.

For Dr. Sallam and his team, *M. shahinae* is only the beginning to understanding African dinosaurs. The paleontologists hope to make another find. Where they found the huge herbivore, they also hope to find the carnivore

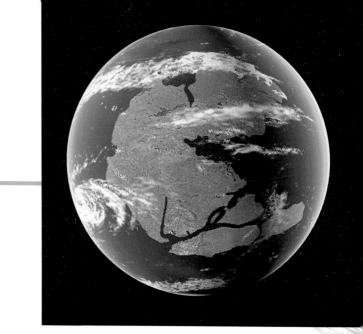

GONDWANA

Three hundred MYA, the continents as seen on Earth today did not exist. Instead, there was one large landmass known by scientists as Pangaea (pictured). Scientists believe that this supercontinent sat on several tectonic plates, or slabs of rock that make up the surface of the planet. As these tectonic plates shifted, Pangaea split, and by 200 MYA, there were two continents. Gondwana contained what are now South America, Africa, Australia, and Antarctica. Laurasia included modern North America, Europe, and Asia. The tectonic plates continued to shift, and landmasses moved. The continents have been in their modern positions for less than 65 million years.

that preyed on it. There are many gaps in what scientists know about ancient reptiles, so every piece of information brings them closer to understanding how reptiles evolved.

EVOLUTION

When scientists speak of evolution, they are talking about the physical changes that take place in species over time. These changes don't mean a group of animals is getting better, but they don't mean that the group is getting worse either. They simply mean that a plant or animal species is changing.

The first scientist who published an explanation of evolution was the French naturalist Jean-Baptiste Lamarck in 1809, but it wasn't until 1859 that an accurate description of the process was released. English naturalist Charles Darwin wrote a book called *On the Origin of Species by Means of Natural Selection*.

JEAN-BAPTISTE LAMARCK

In 1809, Jean-Baptiste Lamarck published his theory that individual animals could acquire a trait and pass it down to their offspring. He pointed out that giraffes reach up to feed on tree leaves. Lamarck believed that all of the stretching actually made their necks and limbs longer. When these giraffes had offspring, they passed down these long necks and long legs. It didn't take long for other scientists to disprove this theory. It was clear that a person who has strong arms from hard work does not automatically have a child with strong arms.

In this book, Darwin put forward the idea that nature and survival were the forces through which evolutionary change occurred.

Darwin observed that a species could have a number of diverse traits. Because of these traits, some animals would have an improved chance of survival. They might be better runners or might be better able to blend with the landscape than others. Because they survived longer, they would have more offspring. Many of these offspring would inherit the beneficial traits, survive longer, reproduce more, and pass the traits on again to their own offspring. Generation by generation, the positive traits would be present in more individuals, and the less beneficial traits would slowly disappear as animals with those traits failed to reproduce in large numbers. As certain traits became more common and others less common, the species evolved. But Darwin did not understand how evolution occurred.

A key piece to this puzzle emerged in 1866 when scientist Gregor Mendel published some important rules of heredity. Mendel noted that a tall pea plant bred with a short pea plant produced tall offspring. When he bred two of these offspring, three-fourths of the resulting plants would be tall and one-fourth would be short. Mendel realized that each plant inherited traits from both parents, with certain traits, known as dominant traits, expressed most often. In pea plants, tallness is dominant over shortness. Scientists today know that change also occurs through mutations. Mutations can take place when cells divide. Changes in the DNA cause the production of different proteins. Some mutations end up being advantageous. The animals with these mutations survive and reproduce, and the species evolves.

If a new trait spreads through an entire species, the species as a whole evolves. But sometimes a population of animals or plants is divided. This can happen when water levels rise and create islands. Animals on one island are isolated from those on a different island. The two groups evolve separately. As the changes accumulate, the two groups grow to be so different they become separate species.

This is how more than 10,000 species of reptiles living today evolved from the earliest known reptile, *Hylonomus lyelli*.[4] *Hylonomus lyelli* lived in what is now Canada approximately 350 MYA. It looked like a lizard and was eight inches (20 cm) long.[5] It sheltered in the stumps of fallen trees, where it ate insects and snails. Slowly, over millions of years, as the environment changed and new sources of food became available, *H. lyelli* and its descendants evolved into the crocodiles, snakes, turtles, and lizards that populate Earth today.

A fossil of *H. lyelli* shows the animal's upper jaw and teeth.

REPTILES DEFINED

There are four orders of reptiles. The order Crocodilia includes the crocodiles, alligators, caimans, and gharials. Testudines includes the tortoises, turtles, sea turtles, terrapins, and freshwater soft-shelled turtles. Lizards and snakes make up the order Squamata. The lizard-like tuatara is the only living member of the order Rhynchocephalia.

As different as these reptiles are, they share common traits. One of the first things many people notice about reptiles is their skin. It is dry but may look shiny because it is covered in scales, bony plates, or a combination of the two. Scales and plates make a reptile's skin waterproof.

Most reptiles cannot regulate their body temperatures internally, so they are often called cold blooded. It is more accurate to call them poikilothermic, which means that their body temperatures vary depending on the temperature of their environment. A desert lizard's body temperature rises as the day grows hot, so the lizard returns to its cool, shaded burrow to avoid overheating. When a turtle's temperature drops because it has been swimming in cool water, it suns itself on a log.

Another trait shared by reptiles is how they reproduce. Reptile young hatch from eggs that are fertilized within the female's body. Most reptiles lay these soft-shell eggs in nests that are then buried, allowing the young to mature before hatching. Some reptiles have evolved so that the female keeps eggs with thin shells or membranes inside her body until they hatch. This is called viviparity. While reptiles have many things in common, they have also developed a wide array of sizes, shapes, and traits. Reptiles live in a variety of ecosystems around the world.

African spurred tortoise
Geochelone sulcata

DOMAIN	**Eukaryota**. This domain includes plants, animals, and fungi. These organisms are grouped together because their cells each have a nucleus, a cell structure that contains the DNA.
KINGDOM	**Animalia**. All animals, including mammals and reptiles, are in this group.
PHYLUM	**Chordata**. Organisms in this phylum have a nerve cord down their backs supported by a rod of cartilage at some point in life. All animals with spines, including mammals and fish, are in this group.
CLASS	**Reptilia**. This class contains all reptiles, which lay leathery eggs and often have scales.
ORDER	**Testudines**. This order contains turtles, which have shells.
FAMILY	**Testudinidae**. Tortoises, which live on land in warm climates, make up this family.
GENUS	*Geochelone*. The largest living turtles that dwell on land make up this genus.
SPECIES	*sulcata*. African spurred tortoises are the largest African tortoises that live on the mainland.

Taxonomic classification is the science of identifying living things, grouping them together, and naming them. When this is done, each organism is assigned a place in eight different categories ranging from domain, the most general category, to species, the most specific category. When the scientific name of an animal is given, it includes the genus, which is capitalized, and the species, which is not. African spurred tortoises are *Geochelone sulcata*. Scientific names are often abbreviated after first use: *G. sulcata*.

Scales

Scientists have debated whether there is a relationship between how lizards produce scales, birds produce feathers, and mammals produce hair. In mammals and birds, a placode, or thickened point in the skin, forms. From this placode, the hair or feather sprouts. No placodes are found where scales grow from reptilian skin. For decades, some scientists believed that all three kinds of animals had a gene series for placodes but reptiles did not grow the physical structure. Then in 2016, Michel Milinkovitch, a geneticist from the University of Geneva, worked with a team of scientists to study an Australian bearded dragon with a mutation in the EDA gene that encodes ectodysplasin A. This protein is involved in the development of placodes. The scientists measured the EDA found in the cells of an Australian bearded dragon with normal scales, in the cells of a bearded dragon with smaller-than-normal scales, and in the cells of lizards with no scales. Those with the most EDA had normal scales. Those with none had no scales. Even without visible placodes, the gene seemed to play a role in scale growth. Milinkovitch and his team may have found the starting point for the evolution of scales as well as feathers and fur.

Scales grow on top of many reptiles' skin, keeping them dry.

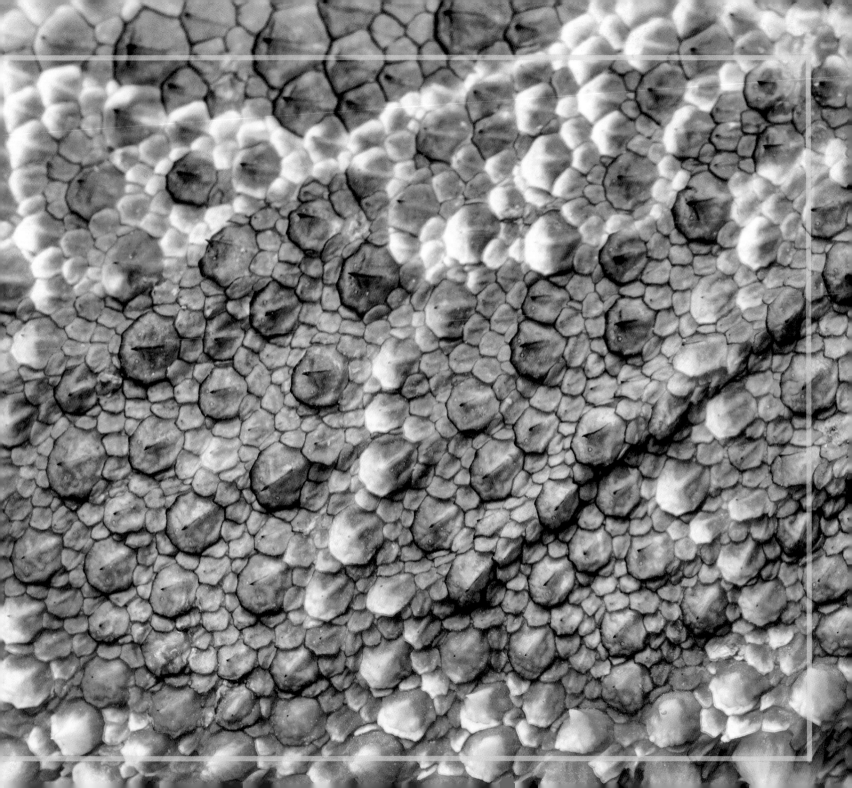

CHAPTER TWO

Tuatara

Sometime between 85 and 80 MYA, the tectonic plates that cover the surface of Earth shifted. New Zealand separated from the continent of Gondwana. The new island was covered by plants typical of Gondwana, including ferns and forests of beech trees and early pine trees. Mammals had not yet established themselves there.

Because of the lack of mammals, animals evolved in New Zealand in ways that would later leave them vulnerable to mammals like invasive rats and stoats. Especially vulnerable are ground-dwelling birds such as the kiwi and the kakapo, a flightless, nocturnal parrot. With limited predators, unique insects also evolved. One of these is the hand-sized weta, with large back legs and curved tusks. But perhaps the most distinctive of all New Zealand animals is the reptile known as the tuatara.

Tuatara eat worms, frogs, snails, and insects, among other things.

SUNKEN NEW ZEALAND

New Zealand, the island nation that exists today, is only a small part of Zealandia, the ancient island that pulled away from Gondwana as a result of plate tectonics. The vast majority of Zealandia, which was the size of modern-day India, lies sunken beneath the Tasman Sea. Some scientists believe that the entire island submerged 25 to 22 MYA and modern New Zealand reemerged later following additional movement of the tectonic plates. If the entire island did submerge, that means that all plant and animal life on New Zealand today migrated and developed since the reemergence of the island. However, there are tuatara fossils that date from before the island would have sunk. And scientists have found three tuatara jaw fragments that are 18 million years old. According to Te Papa museum fossil curator Alan Tennyson, this evidence seems to indicate that some of Zealandia stayed above water, allowing New Zealand's plants and animals to continue living there. He believes it is unlikely tuatara lived on the island before submersion, died off, and reestablished themselves in only a few million years.

Tuatara look like lizards, although they are different in several ways. Lizards have a smooth membrane on either side of their heads. These are their external ears. Tuatara have no external ears. While most lizards are active during the day, tuatara are active at night because they can handle cooler temperatures than lizards. Unlike lizards, which are part of the order Squamata, tuatara are the last surviving member of the order Rhynchocephalia.

RHYNCHOCEPHALIA

Because tuatara are the only living rhynchocephalians, many people mistakenly assume that the group is primitive and unsuccessful. Rhynchocephalians emerged during the middle of the Triassic

The tuatara's tolerance of the cold allows it to live in climates many reptiles cannot.

period (251.9–201.3 MYA). In the last 30 years, scientific research has shown that as recently as the Cretaceous, this group had diversified and filled a wide variety of niches.

One example of this diversity is *Ankylosphenodon*, which lived in central Mexico at the end of the early part of the Cretaceous. Unlike the modern tuatara, the shape of *Ankylosphenodon*'s teeth and jaw suggest to scientists that this ancient rhynchocephalian was herbivorous. Instead of evolving heavier enamel to withstand the wear of chewing plants, *Ankylosphenodon* evolved to replace old worn teeth with new ones. These animals were also aquatic, having evolved heavy ribs to help keep their lungs from collapsing due to the water pressure. Their ribs also provided the weight needed to help them dive.

LONG LIVES

Scientists are studying tuatara in the wild. They tag individual animals, giving the scientists an idea of how old these animals are when they're recaptured. "Tuataras routinely live to 100, and I couldn't tell you they don't live to 150, 200 years or even more," said Dr. Charles Daugherty from Victoria University of Wellington in New Zealand. "We know there are females that are still reproducing in their 80s." One captive tuatara became a first-time father at 111 years old.[1]

The group declined during the late part of the Cretaceous. No fossil evidence has been found to explain this decline. Many scientists believe the rhynchocephalians declined as the squamates—lizards and snakes—diversified. In their geographically isolated niche, the tuatara survived.

TUATARA TODAY

Modern tuatara are approximately 20 inches (50 cm) long and have evolved a number of unique features.[2] The animals have a third eye on top of their heads. In young animals this parietal eye can be seen under the skin, but it is invisible once the animal's adult scales cover this spot. The parietal eye consists of nerve endings, a lenslike structure, and the retina, which detects light. Tuatara do not see shapes or movement with this eye, but scientists believe they can use it to sense light levels.

Tuatara have also evolved a unique set of teeth perfect for crunching up insects as well as the occasional lizard, bird, or bird egg. One of their usual foods is the giant weta. The tuatara's top jaw features two rows of teeth, one behind the other. The lower jaw has a single row of teeth that fits between the upper rows of teeth whenever the animal closes its jaws. The tuatara's teeth are much like those of dinosaurs because they grow directly from the jawbone. Unlike in

The giant weta is the biggest insect in the world.

mammals, there is no tooth socket in which the tooth nests. Because of their primitive teeth and the third eye, some people call tuatara living fossils.

Tuatara take a long time to reproduce. Males can mate every year, but females most often mate only every two to five years. Mating takes place in March each year. Approximately ten months after the female mates, she lays one to 19 eggs in a specially dug nest chamber. After being covered, the eggs may be guarded for a week or two but are then left unguarded and may take more than a year to hatch, during which time they are vulnerable to rats and other predators.[3] As with some other reptiles, including crocodiles, the temperature of the nesting burrow determines the gender of the offspring. Temperatures a single degree too warm can mean a clutch will be entirely male. This could become problematic given the rising temperatures caused by climate change.

Tuatara also have unique hemoglobin, a protein in red blood cells that helps move oxygen from the lungs to tissues. The unique hemoglobin allows tuatara to be active at night when dropping temperatures force other reptiles to become inactive. Even when the temperature is only 45 to 46 degrees Fahrenheit (7–8°C), which would kill most reptiles, some tuatara remain active.[4]

RAPID EVOLUTION?

The tuatara may take a long time to hatch and grow, but some New Zealand scientists think this reptile may actually evolve faster than many animals. In March 2008, David Lambert from New Zealand's Massey University and his fellow researchers published an article on tuatara genetics in the journal *Trends in Genetics*. The group had sampled DNA from 33 fossils that were up to 8,750 years old, as well as the DNA of 41 modern tuatara.[5]

They found that the tuatara had the highest rate of evolution of any animal ever studied. DNA is made of four different chemicals called bases. In DNA's double strands, these bases always pair up. The chemical adenine in one strand pairs with thymine in the other. Guanine pairs with cytosine. A mutation occurs when, during DNA's duplication in the making of sperm or eggs, one base pair is substituted for

FAST FOSSILS

Critics of David Lambert's work contest the use of fossil DNA in calculating the rate of tuatara evolution. They say that when ancient DNA is used in an analysis, rates of change frequently score much higher than when only modern DNA is used. "Both estimates cannot be correct," says David Hillis of the University of Texas in Austin. "It is a lot easier for me to think of reasons why the ancient DNA comparisons might be suspect than the reverse."[6] Errors could happen because of damage to ancient DNA due to long-term exposure to the elements.

Conservationists are trying to protect the tuatara for future generations.

another. The researchers' comparison returned an estimate of 1.56 sequence changes per base every million years. This is three times faster than mutations occur in brown bears.[7] However, many scientists do not agree with Lambert's conclusions.

Lambert is concerned for the survival of the tuatara. Despite this rapid change at the genetic level, the tuatara has changed very little physically. Exactly what this DNA controls is still a mystery. In the near future, physical change may be necessary to ensure survival. Since warmer temperatures will skew the tuatara's population toward having more males, these temperatures will likely reduce their reproductive success.

CHAPTER THREE

Turtles

In South Africa 260 MYA, a broad-bodied animal that looked like a lizard burrowed into the riverbanks. Its powerful front legs tore into the soil as it dug down. The *Eunotosaurus* looked like a lizard, but Tyler Lyson, the curator of vertebrate paleontology at the Denver Museum of Science and Nature, has identified it as one of the earliest turtles. He says that its wide ribs finally provide the answer to how turtles evolved their bulky shells.

For a long time, paleontologists believed that turtles developed their shells strictly for defense. They were also certain that shells evolved from osteoderms, the bony plates that make up the armor found on crocodiles, armadillos, and some dinosaurs, including *M. shahinae*. Scientists believed that over time, osteoderms broadened and fused together, becoming the turtle's shell.

No other animals have shells with the same structure as a turtle's shell.

Biologists who studied modern turtle embryos had another theory. They made observations as turtle embryos developed. What they saw convinced them that the shell instead evolved from ribs that had broadened out.

Then, in 2008, Chinese researchers discovered a 220-million-year-old turtle fossil. They named their find *Odontochelys semitestacea*, meaning "toothed turtle in a half shell." This fossil had no osteoderms and no carapace. But it did have a shell that covered its belly, and it also had broad ribs. With this find, researchers learned to look for broad ribs to find ancient turtles.

That's what led Lyson to the *Eunotosaurus*, originally discovered in 1892. When Lyson examined a number of *Eunotosaurus* fossils, he found the traits of a digging creature, including dense forelimb bones and ridges in its bones that showed where well-developed muscles would have attached. The broad ribs also helped in this activity, anchoring the reptile's muscles.

SWIMMER OR DIGGER?

When Tyler Lyson studied *Eunotosaurus*, he saw features that could evolve to help an animal swim or dig. Its front feet were larger and stronger than its back feet. It had shoulder blades and forelegs with pronounced attachments for large, strong muscles so it could pull back its front limbs with great strength. But *Eunotosaurus* also had two features only diggers have—clawed front feet to break up the soil and thick, heavy bones to handle the force needed to dig.

In 2015, a new find added another ancient turtle to the lineage. Rainer R. Schoch from the Natural History Museum in Stuttgart, Germany, and Hans-Dieter Sues at the Smithsonian's National Museum of Natural History in Washington, DC, discovered *Pappochelys* in southern Germany. This box turtle–sized animal lived 240 MYA on the shores of an ancient lake. Although it still had no carapace, it had broad ribs like *Eunotosaurus*, as well as a row of shell-like bones along its belly.

Broad ribs support digging muscles, but they also slow an animal down. Reptiles bend their bodies from side to side to lengthen their strides. Wide ribs would limit this undulating movement, much as a turtle's shell does today. Like modern turtles, these ancient wide-ribbed animals would walk with only the motion of their legs, making them slow. Lyson believes this slow gait is what made the evolution of the full protective shell necessary.

CONVERGENT EVOLUTION

Not all animals that live in similar ways and develop similar features are closely related. Convergent evolution is the process through which two animals from different scientific families evolve in similar ways. Some tortoises use their strong leg muscles to dig for insect meals or to dig burrows. Their armored shells provide protection. But not every armored digger that lives in a burrow and eats insects is a tortoise or even a reptile. One mammal that fits this description is the armadillo, whose name is Spanish for "little armored one."

The Museum
am Löwentor
in Germany
houses a fossil
of *Pappochelys*.

Judy Cebra-Thomas, an associate professor of developmental biology at Millersville University in Lancaster, Pennsylvania, agrees: "The selective pressure to develop protective structures may have come from the slower gait that resulted from the broader ribs."[1] In this way, the turtle's shell is an example of exaptation, in which a trait evolves for one purpose and then evolves further to solve another need. In this case, the trait that initially worked well for digging was later used for defense.

TURTLES TAKE TO WATER

Until recently, scientists had been having a hard time estimating when sea turtles separated from freshwater turtles. Part of the problem is that it is hard to recognize a turtle fossil as a sea turtle. One of the defining traits of sea turtles, the salt glands, does not fossilize because these glands are soft tissue. Despite this, a study published in 2015 was able to estimate when this split occurred.

In 2015, Edwin Cadena of the Senckenberg Research Institute in Frankfurt, Germany, and fellow paleontologist James Parham of California State University, Fullerton, published an article in the journal *PaleoBios* about the oldest known sea turtle fossil, *Desmatochelys padillai*. Mary

Luz Parra, an amateur paleontologist, and her brothers, Juan and Freddy, found *D. padillai* in 2007 in Villa de Leyva, Colombia.

When Cadena and Parham later examined the fossil, they realized that they were looking at something important. *Desmatochelys padillai* is 120 million years old. Even without the salt glands, the scientists identified this fossil as a sea turtle because of the shape and features of its skull and paddle-like front flippers. This 6.5-foot- (2 m) long turtle may well have been prey because the fossilized shell includes two bite marks, probably from a pliosaur.[2] This important fossil not only reveals details about the lives of ancient sea turtles but also is 25 million years older than the next-oldest fossil, pushing back the date when freshwater and sea turtles split.

LOVED TO DEATH

Unfortunately, small turtles with eye-catching shells, such as ornate box turtles, can attract people's attention. Because they are slow moving and easy to catch, people may take these turtles home as pets. People often believe their pet box turtle is healthy, since a well-cared-for ornate box turtle can live 40 years in captivity, but a wild turtle can live to be 100 years old.[3] Turtles are hard to keep in captivity because indoors they may not get the sunlight they need to be healthy. Those kept outdoors may not have an area into which they can burrow for safety. It can also be difficult to provide a turtle with the varied diet needed for good health.

Turtles have low rates of reproduction. This means that taking a turtle out of its home range disrupts the population. Ornate box turtles have few predators, so the greatest threats are people who might capture a turtle to keep it as a pet or accidentally run a turtle down when it is trying to cross a busy road.

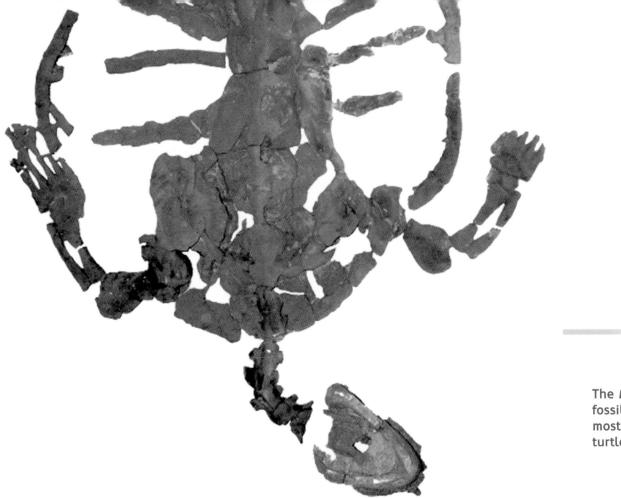

The *D. padillai* fossil is one of the most complete sea turtle fossils.

MODERN TURTLES, TORTOISES, AND TERRAPINS

There are more than 300 species of Testudines living today.[4] This diverse family of animals can be found on every continent except Antarctica. Although people call all of the animals in this order turtles, scientifically the term *turtle* is properly used to describe modern animals

Today, many sea turtles are in danger of extinction.

that spend most of their lives in water. Also in this family are the land-dwelling tortoises and terrapins, which spend time both on land and in the water.

Turtles have adapted to this aquatic life with streamlined bodies and either webbed feet like a snapping turtle or flippers like a sea turtle. They live in salt and fresh water and come onto land only to lay their eggs in nests they have dug. Freshwater turtles may also come out of the water to sun themselves on rocks or logs. The largest is the leatherback turtle, a type of sea turtle that weighs up to 1,500 pounds (680 kg).[5]

Tortoises are land animals. Adapted for walking on land, they have rounded feet with claws. Like their ancestors, tortoises dig

TOLERATING THE COLD

Box turtles survive winter temperatures by taking shelter in overwintering burrows. Air temperatures are often colder than ground temperatures. In areas with mild temperatures, box turtles may dig barely deep enough to cover their shells, but in colder areas they dig much deeper. In Wisconsin, one female box turtle was found in a burrow 3.6 feet (1.1 m) deep. Females dig holes to lay their eggs in. When turtles hatch from the eggs in the fall, they do not remain in the nesting burrow, which is too near the surface to protect them from winter cold. Instead, they dig a new burrow beneath the nesting burrow up to 2.2 feet (0.68 m) deep.[6]

American desert tortoises have many adaptations that allow them to live in dry, hot places.

burrows to find shelter, often using these burrows to help regulate their body temperature.

The American desert tortoise spends much of its time underground. When it feeds on flowers and grasses during the rainy season, it stores the water from these foods in its body. It can live for a year without drinking water. During the dry season, it has a period where it is inactive. Remaining in its burrow protects it from the extreme heat and helps it conserve water.

Diamondback terrapins are named for the diamond-like designs on the backs of their shells.

Terrapins spend their lives both on land and in the water. They live in swamps, ponds, lakes, and streams. Diamondback terrapins live throughout much of the eastern coastal states of the United States. They are capable of going dormant in cold weather. They have adapted a ridge in their mouths to help them crush the shellfish that make up a large part of their diet. On land and in water, turtles, tortoises, and terrapins have adapted to a variety of niches around the world.

CHAPTER FOUR

Crocodilians

Today, there are 23 species of crocodilians swimming in fresh and salt waters around the world. They have powerful jaws, cone-shaped teeth, and four short legs ending in feet with webbed toes. Their eyes and nose can stay above water while the rest of their heads and bodies are submerged. The largest is the saltwater crocodile, which reaches up to 20 feet (6 m) long.[1] The smallest is the smooth-fronted caiman, only 3.9 to 4.9 feet (1.2–1.5 m) long.[2] Crocodilians live on every continent except Antarctica and Europe.

Like most reptiles, crocodilians lay eggs in nests on land. When young crocodilians hatch, they stay together near the nest because they are small enough to be prey. Although adults are safe from most predators, both fish and birds will eat the hatchlings. They reach

A crocodile can often be distinguished from an alligator by the fourth tooth on its lower jaw, which overlaps the upper jaw. Lower teeth are hidden on an alligator.

adulthood in approximately ten years. American crocodiles live to be 50 to 75 years old in the wild. Scientists estimate that Nile crocodiles can live as long as 80 years, while alligators and caimans live from 30 to 60 years in the wild.[3]

Crocodilians are ambush hunters who will eat almost anything. When they are young and small, their diet includes fish, frogs, and crustaceans. When they reach maturity, they eat mostly fish and some mammals that come into the water. To make it easier to hunt at night or in murky water, they have evolved pits along their mouths. These pits contain receptors that detect the movement of potential prey, even when this prey cannot be seen.

DIETARY VARIETY

Paul Sereno, a paleontologist at the University of Chicago, has searched the Sahara Desert since the 1990s for ancestors of the crocodiles. Some of the animals he has found lived as long as 110 MYA. Sereno has found fossils with projecting teeth in the lower jaw. He believes these teeth may have helped the animals dig up tubers, or roots, as part of their diet. Another find had a broad, droopy snout and hooked teeth that may have helped it catch small fish and worms in shallow water.

Crocodilians have a reputation as people eaters. For the Nile crocodile, that may be deserved. Up to 200 deaths a year are reported, but scientists don't think that Nile crocodiles seek out people to hunt.[4] Crocodilians are opportunists, striking when something moves nearby, whether it is a young wildebeest coming to drink or a person coming to wash clothes in the river. People and Nile crocodiles frequently live close to each other, which increases the chances for humans to encounter these 16-foot (4.9 m) predators.[5]

Unlike the Nile crocodile, India's gharial, which is sometimes called the gavial, is critically endangered. This is because many wetland areas in which it once lived have dried out because people altered river courses. Unlike other crocodilians, gharials do not lunge at prey. Instead, they move their heads from side to side in the water to capture fish.

American alligators live only in the wetlands of the southeastern United States. They reach an average size of 10 to 15 feet (3 to 4.5 m). At one time, this animal was endangered. Efforts to

GHARIAL

The gharial is sexually dimorphic. This means that the males and females look different. Males are much bigger than females: 16.5 to 19.7 feet (5–6 m) long compared with females at 12.25 to 15.5 feet (3.7–4.7 m).[6] A mature male gharial has a ghara, or fleshy bulb (pictured), on the end of his snout. Scientists believe that its purpose is to signal to females that he is able to mate. Instead of hissing like females and immature males, the adult male is able to use the ghara as a sound chamber to turn its hiss into an easily recognizable buzzing noise.

preserve its habitat, as well as hunting laws, have increased its wild population to more than one million animals.[7]

Caimans live in Central and South America. The largest caiman is the sometimes-aggressive black caiman, which can be up to 15 feet (4.5 m) long.[8] The smooth-fronted caiman is the smallest. This caiman lives in fast-moving streams in the Amazon and feeds on fish, birds, insects, and other small animals.

With their elongated bodies, crocodilians have adapted to their aquatic lifestyles. Their tails are long and muscular for propelling them forward through the water. With a series of nasal flaps, these reptiles can hold their breath even when their mouths are open underwater. In addition to their upper and lower eyelids, they have a translucent membrane over their eyes that can be closed when the animal is underwater. This allows the animal to see while protecting its eyes from debris floating in the water.

UNRECOGNIZABLE ANCESTORS

Long before the crocodilians evolved their distinctive streamlined, short-legged body, they lived on land. Some were herbivores, but many were hunters. During the middle of the Triassic, *Carnufex* hunted in the swamps of North America. Similar to many early crocodilians, *Carnufex*

An ancient relative of the crocodile, *Postosuchus* had shorter front legs than hind legs and was faster on land than a crocodile.

was bipedal, walking upright on two legs like a small *Tyrannosaurus rex*. It was approximately nine feet (2.7 m) long and weighed 500 pounds (230 kg).[9] Scientists think it may have been the apex, or top, predator in its ecosystem. It most likely ate small mammals and other prehistoric reptiles.

Baurusuchus lived in South America during the middle to late parts of the Cretaceous. Unlike *Carnufex*, *Baurusuchus* didn't even occupy a semiaquatic habitat. Its heavy skull shows it had strong jaw muscles with nostrils located on the front of its snout like a dog's, instead of on top of the snout like a modern crocodile's. Scientists believe that this long-legged predator ran across the plains of South America in search of prey.

STOMATOSUCHUS

Stomatosuchus lived during the late part of the Cretaceous in Egypt. It is known only by the fossil of a single skull, which was destroyed in 1944 during World War II (1939–1945). Its snout was long and flat, with a broad upper jaw resembling a lid. Short, cone-shaped teeth may have been found in only the upper jaw, and the animal may have had a throat pouch. Some scientists believe it may have eaten krill, tiny shrimp, which animals such as the modern blue whale eat today.

It was on land that crocodiles evolved the massive jaws they use to capture prey. In 2004, James Clark, an associate professor of biology at George Washington University in Washington, DC, published an article in the journal *Nature*. Clark and his coauthors described a fossil they found in China. *Junggarsuchus sloani* lived from 230 to 150 MYA and was only approximately three feet (1 m) long.[10] Its legs, positioned beneath its body much like a modern dog's, were adapted for running on land. They were unlike the short legs of a modern crocodile, which fold back against the animal's sides when it swims. Yet *J. sloani*'s skull and teeth had already adapted for the swift bite of the modern crocodile.

GENOME REVELATIONS

In 2014, a team of scientists from the University of California, Santa Cruz, completed a study of the crocodilian genome. They sequenced the genes of an American alligator, a saltwater crocodile, and a gharial. Genes are made up of four chemical building blocks, known as bases. When scientists sequence a gene, they map out the order in which these bases appear in a sample of genetic material. These maps allowed the scientists to compare the crocodilian genomes with recently published bird genomes. As so often happens when scientists study genes compared with how an animal looks, the results contained a few surprises. Crocodiles are related to lizards, but they are even more closely related to birds.

The study revealed that crocodiles, birds, and dinosaurs had a common ancestor 240 MYA. This ancestor is called the archosaur, meaning "ruling lizard." When birds and dinosaurs separated from crocodilians, they were all bipedal.

Reconstructing the genetic timeline was made easier by the fact that crocodiles have evolved so slowly. "We can see back into their past more cleanly," said Richard E. Green, lead

An artist depicts what an archosaur may have looked like.

author of the crocodilian genome paper and an assistant professor of biomolecular engineering at the University of California, Santa Cruz.[11] Green believes that part of the reason for this slower evolution is the length of time it takes for crocodilians to mature sexually and then reproduce.

"When it takes longer to get from one generation to the next, you expect the evolutionary rate to be slower, and big animals tend to have long generation times," he said. "We know from fossils that the body plan of crocs has remained largely unchanged for millions of years. Mammals, however, if you go back 50 or 60 million years there were no big mammals, so we see a faster rate of evolutionary change."[12]

Birds, which take less time to mature and reproduce than crocodilians, have a much faster rate of evolutionary change. This is part of the reason why, after a mass extinction 66 MYA that wiped out the dinosaurs, birds not only survived but rapidly diversified. Evolution takes place in fewer years when a generation lives and reproduces in a shorter amount of time.

GENOME 10K

The study of the crocodilian genome is part of the Genome 10K project. The goal of the Genome 10K project is to sequence the genomes of at least one individual from each vertebrate genus, totaling approximately 10,000 genomes. The founders of the Genome 10K project want to help scientists better understand how animal life evolved, and they believe that the best way to do this is through the study of DNA. "G10K's contributions include a lot of work convincing people to work together, setting up collaborations, and holding meetings to get people to share ideas and get to know each other," said David Haussler, who is one of the organizers and a professor of biomolecular engineering and director of the Genomics Institute at the University of California, Santa Cruz.[13] Genome 10K is one of a growing number of scientific endeavors that emphasize international cooperation and assistance.

CHAPTER FIVE

Snakes

More than 3,700 species of snakes have been identified, but very little is known about their evolution.[1] A big part of the problem is that snakes have fragile skeletons with slender bones. Not every skeleton fossilizes, and smaller bones are less likely to survive long enough to fossilize.

Some scientists once thought snakes descended from mosasaurs. Mosasaurs are a group of marine reptiles that appeared in the fossil record 100 MYA. The theory that snakes are descended from mosasaurs is based on phylogeny, the study of how organisms are related, often based on physical appearance. Physically, scientists found similarities in the skulls and jaws of mosasaurs and snakes. Both have hinged jaws that allow the mouths to open extra wide to swallow large prey. Both snakes and mosasaurs also have teeth

Snake fossils are relatively rare but valuable to learning more about their evolution.

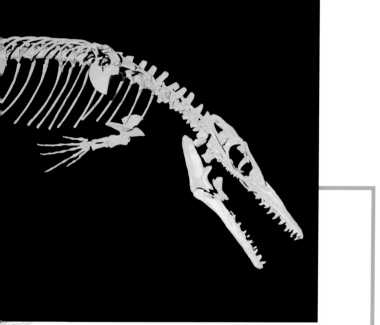

MOSASAURUS

During the Mesozoic era, which began with the Triassic and ended with the Cretaceous, marine reptiles known as mosasaurs (pictured) dominated the sea. One of the oldest mosasaur fossils discovered was a skull from the chalk deposits of Maastricht, Netherlands. It was found in 1764. Mosasaurs could grow to more than 30 feet (9 m) long.[3] They dined on turtles, sharks, and even other mosasaurs. Some smaller mosasaurs had rounded teeth adapted for crunching shellfish. There were both whale-sized species and slender, fast-moving, ambush-hunting species. Mosasaur placement in the reptile family tree is uncertain.

on the roofs of their mouths to keep prey from escaping. Mosasaurs and some snakes also give birth to live young instead of laying eggs. However, certain finds offer evidence against the connection between snakes and mosasaurs.

In 2004, Michael Caldwell, a professor in the department of biological sciences at the University of Alberta in Canada, was at the Natural History Museum in London. He saw a fossil of a maxilla, or upper jaw, that in the 1990s had been classified as a lizard. "When I looked at this specimen . . . with my snake-comparative-anatomy hat on, it was really very, very obvious that it was a snake maxilla," Caldwell explains. The fossil was reclassified as a 143-million-year-old *Parviraptor estesi*.[2] This is one of the oldest snake fossils.

LAND-BOUND ANCESTORS

Scientists' updated theory is that small burrowing lizards were the ancestors of modern snakes. Many scientists believe the ancestor is an as-yet-unidentified land-dwelling, four-legged lizard of the early Cretaceous. It probably burrowed, and it is closely related to the monitor lizards of today.

David Martill, a professor of paleobiology at the University of Portsmouth in the United Kingdom, believes he found a transitional species, one of the species between the full lizard and full snake. In 2015, Martill spotted the fossil of *Tetrapodophis amplectus* at the museum in Solnhofen, Germany. He later returned with paleontologists Nicholas R. Longrich and Helmut Tischlinger to study the fossil. It had been found in a Brazilian geological formation from the early part of the Cretaceous. They think it is a transition species because it has lizard traits such as four limbs as well as snake traits such as backward-slanted teeth.

HEAD FIRST OR BODY FIRST?

Some theories on snake evolution propose an unequal rate of development, with either a snakelike body or a compact head developing first. The research done at the University of Helsinki did not favor either a head-first or body-first picture of snake evolution. Instead, the findings from this research group suggest that the body and head developed simultaneously, although additional research is needed to prove this theory.

CONTROVERSY

Not all scientists accept that *T. amplectus* is a snake ancestor. One of the scientists asking questions is Michael Caldwell. He claims the fossil does not show any of the features a scientist would expect to see in a snake. For one, snakes evolved teeth that hook backwards to help keep prey from pulling free. *Tetrapodophis amplectus* does not have these hooked teeth. Snakes also have a ridge along the base of their teeth, which *T. amplectus* does not have. Last but not least, snakes also have zygosphenes, a part on each vertebra that juts out and fits into a notch in the next vertebra. *Tetrapodophis amplectus* does not have these features either. Caldwell believes *T. amplectus* is a *Dolichosaurus*, an ancient reptile that is related to snakes but is not an ancestor to them. Scientists are not yet certain where *Dolichosaurus* fits into the reptilian family tree.

Tetrapodophis amplectus isn't the only possible transition species. Three ancient snakes, *Eupodophis*, *Haasiophis*, and *Pachyrhachis* from the Middle East, as well as one, *Najash*, from South America, all have tiny, nonfunctioning hind legs. Some scientists believe that one of them may be the ancestor of today's snakes.

SKULL STRUCTURE

In an attempt to determine how and where snakes evolved, researchers at the University of Helsinki in Finland compared skull shape and size with the habitats in which the animals live. They approached natural history museums and digital morphology libraries that keep digital scans of various animals, as well as paleontologists, biologists, and herpetologists from around the world. With help from these organizations and individuals, the team from Helsinki accessed more than 300 species of tuatara, lizards, and snakes, including skulls from modern adults and embryonic animals, as well as fossils.[4]

Once the researchers had the specimens, they compared the skulls. They discovered that over time, lizards evolved to become fossorial, or adapted for burrowing, and they became longer and thinner. These animals eventually lost their legs, and their skulls grew smaller and more flexible.

Seeing this consistent pattern, the researchers became convinced that lizards transitioned to snakes—not in the water, not above ground, but underground. There, their bodies elongated, their limbs vanished, and their skulls became smaller and rigid. Based on skull size and design, the researchers believe that snakes first adapted to underground ecosystems. Only then did snakes move into the diverse habitats, underground, above ground, and aquatic, where they are found today.

MODERN SNAKES

There are more than 3,700 different species of snakes. Of these, more than 700 are venomous.[5] Snakes are rare in the Arctic and have never lived in Antarctica or Ireland. Rarely, a sea snake will be seen off the coast of New Zealand. With these exceptions, snakes can be found all around the world in a variety of habitats, although warmer environments are easier for them to adapt to than colder ones. Snakes are common in tropical forests and grasslands, as well as in semiaquatic environments such as wetlands and marshes.

Despite their lack of limbs, snakes move easily because of specially adapted scales. Called ventral scutes, a single row of these flattened, narrow scales runs the length of every snake's belly. The scutes on faster-moving species extend partway up the animal's sides.

Snakes have no eyelids, so they cannot blink or close their eyes. In sleep, they narrow their pupils to reduce how much light can enter them. This makes it very hard to tell when a snake is sleeping. Snakes have a spectacle, or special transparent scale, over each eye. One

SNAKE EYES

Both the anatomy and genetics of vision have been thoroughly studied in mammals, birds, and fish. Vision in reptiles has received much less attention. Anatomical studies of snakes' eyes show that the rods, which are cells that see at low light levels, and cones, cells that detect color, are diverse and highly evolved. The study showed that some snakes can see UV light, something that is very helpful for animals that hunt in low light conditions. Understanding how and why this ability evolved will only be possible with further research.

Scutes help snakes
move on many
kinds of surfaces,
including branches.

study of snake vision revealed that the eyes of snakes that hunt during the day filter out harmful ultraviolet (UV) light, much like sunglasses.

Snakes have also adapted special ways to hunt and defend themselves. Approximately 30 species of cobra live in the forests, grasslands, woods, and rocky hillsides of Africa and Asia.[6] While the word *cobra* typically refers to snakes in the genus *Naja*, some people use it to refer to a few other types of snakes as well. To capture prey, cobras bite the animal and inject venom. When a cobra feels threatened, a special group of ribs flares outward and opens the cobra's hood. This makes the snake look bigger.

Another type of snake that has evolved venom to hunt is the rattlesnake, of which there are approximately 50 species.[7] A rattlesnake's first line of defense is protective coloration that helps it hide in the rocky, sandy, or leaf-littered environments where it lives. In addition to camouflage, rattlesnakes have a rattle made of keratin, the same material that makes up human fingernails. When approached, the snake shakes the rattle on the tip of its tail, making a buzzing sound. A snake's last line of defense is to bite, which it also does when it hunts. Unlike other snakes, rattlesnakes can control the amount of venom injected.

Rattlesnakes may use their tails to warn away hikers who get too close.

Not all snakes hunt using venom. The green anaconda of South America is a constrictor that squeezes its prey. It is the world's heaviest snake and tends to spend time in the water since water supports its large body. The eyes and nostrils of this snake are on the top of its head, enabling it to wait almost entirely submerged for prey such as wild pigs, caimans, deer, turtles, and even jaguars. It wraps around its prey and squeezes, constricting the prey to death. Like other snakes, the anaconda has a jaw adaptation, with the upper and lower jaws attached by stretchy ligaments that allow the jaws to separate so that the snake can swallow large prey.

CHAPTER SIX

Geckos

In March 2016, scientists published a paper in the journal *Science Advances* about a group of 12 fossilized lizards trapped in amber.[1] Amber is a type of fossilized tree resin. When the bark of certain trees is cut or torn, the tree produces a special resin to seal the break and kill any germs. Some tree species produce so much of this resin that it can trap an insect or other small animal. If the resin is a type that is chemically stable, meaning that it will not decompose, and it is buried in sediment, it can fossilize. If the resin has trapped some small animal, that too will fossilize. The 12 lizards in amber were found decades earlier, but private collectors own the fossils and only in the 2010s made the pieces available for study. Using computed tomography (CT) scanners to image the fossils, the researchers could

Geckos come in many bright colors.

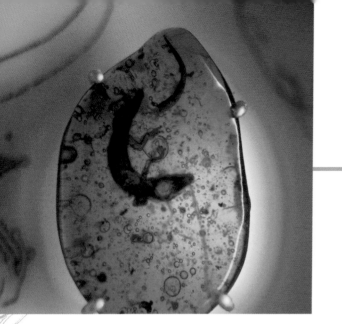

IMPORTANCE OF AMBER

Scientists aren't surprised that a wide variety of lizards, including the 12 lizards in amber, lived in what is now Burma 100 MYA. "There's a fair amount of diversity in the tropics now, so it's not too surprising that they've been diverse in the past," says Kevin de Queiroz, curator of reptiles and amphibians at the Smithsonian's National Museum of Natural History.[2] But the fossil record contains more large animals than smaller ones. Large animals that live in deserts or near riverbeds are the most likely to fossilize. Small animals that live in the moist, hot tropics generally don't fossilize unless they are trapped in resin such as amber. This makes amber fossils scientifically important.

digitally cross-section the lizards, creating scans that look like slices of the fossil without harming the specimens.

Dating the amber told scientists that the lizards were 100 million years old and from the Cretaceous. They had lived at approximately the time scientists believed that lizards first evolved, adapting to niches alongside dinosaurs. Lizards are small and do not often fossilize, so these amber fossils gave the scientists an opportunity to study something rare from a vital period in lizard evolution.

One of the fossils is a gecko. This identification was made because the animal's foot is so well preserved that scientists can see the adhesive toe pads for which geckos are known. This isn't an early version of the gecko toe pad but rather the same design that is seen in the modern lizard. This means that these pads and the gecko's abilities as a climber evolved much earlier than previously thought, which pushed back the date when scientists believe lizards diversified.

GECKOS

Approximately 1,700 species of gecko live on Earth today.[3] These lizards have adapted to live in nearly every kind of environment, ranging from rain forests to deserts. They live on every continent except Antarctica. Most often they eat insects, but quite a few also eat fruit and the nectar from flowers. Some have adapted to store fat in their tails when food is plentiful and use these fat stores when they can't otherwise find the food they need to survive.

Geckos range widely in size. The smallest lizard in the world is the dwarf gecko, which lives on an island in the Dominican Republic. It is only approximately 0.6 inches (1.6 cm) long. One of the largest geckos is the New Caledonian giant gecko, which can grow up to 17 inches (43 cm) long and lives in the New Caledonian islands in the South Pacific.[4]

Geckos have many unique adaptations, including the way they stay clean. The box-patterned gecko is covered in tiny hairlike spines. These spines make the surface of the

Gecko toes are specially adapted for climbing.

gecko very bumpy so that, instead of clinging to the gecko, water beads up and rolls off the gecko's skin. As it does, it carries dust and dirt with it.

Many geckos also have adhesive toe pads. With these pads, geckos that live among trees or rocks or even in people's houses can climb away from predators or toward food such as spiders and moths. Geckos with toe pads have hundreds of thousands of microscopic hairs, called setae, on the underside of their toes. The tip of each seta splits into numerous bristles. These smaller bristles are called spatulae. They are so tiny that they follow the contours of whatever the gecko is standing on closely enough that electrons from the gecko's spatulae and electrons from the surface create a physical bond. By changing the angle of the spatulae, the gecko can turn this ability to cling on and off so quickly that it can run across a ceiling.

GECKO GENOME

In 2015, Huanming Yang at Beijing Genomics Institute and Xiaosong Gu at Nantong University in China headed a team of scientists who published a paper about their work sequencing the first gecko genome. They sequenced the Japanese gecko and identified more than 22,000 genes. The sequenced genome is 2.55 gigabytes in size, approximately 50 percent larger than that of the *Anolis carolinensis* lizard, which had previously been the largest known reptilian genome.[5]

AGAIN AND AGAIN

Only approximately 60 percent of all gecko species have toe pads that allow them to climb walls and other vertical surfaces. To study the evolution of this trait, University of Minnesota postdoctoral researcher Tony Gamble and other scientists created the most complete gecko family tree ever developed. As they grouped the various geckos, they studied which ones had toe pads, which didn't, and where they lived. Working under lead researcher Aaron Bauer, a professor at Villanova University, the scientists found that 11 groups of geckos independently developed sticky toe pads when they lived in areas in which toe pads were beneficial, such as on boulders or in trees. Nine of these groups later lost their toe pads when the adaptation no longer proved beneficial. "The loss of adhesive pads in dune-dwelling species is an excellent example of natural selection in action," Bauer says. In dunes, the toe pads put the lizard at a disadvantage. "Scientists have long thought that adhesive toepads originated just once in geckos, twice at the most," says Gamble. "To discover that geckos evolved sticky toepads again and again is amazing."[7]

Comparing this gecko genome with those of other reptiles, the researchers looked at the similarities and differences. Similarities reveal common ancestry. Differences show the order in which species diverged. These patterns allowed scientists to determine that geckos diverged from other lizards approximately 200 MYA.

In addition to sequencing the genome, the researchers looked for clues on how geckos' toe pads evolved. The team found that the gecko had at least 35 separate genes for setae beta-keratins, the proteins needed to build the setae on its toes. This is nearly twice the number of beta-keratin genes in the *A. carolinensis*.[6] The number suggests that the gecko had to evolve to have a greater number of the genes that produce beta-keratin in order to develop its unique climbing ability.[8]

HUMAN INFLUENCE

In 1996, the Serra da Mesa Dam in Brazil had been completed. The structure was designed to generate hydroelectric power, which is energy harnessed from water flow. By 1998, the reservoir behind the dam had filled, flooding 650 acres (260 ha) and creating nearly 300 hilltop islands.[9] By altering the environment so radically, the dam gave scientists an opportunity to observe what happened to the plants and animals that live in isolated populations.

Before the islands were created, a wide variety of termite-eating lizards lived in the area. Stranded on the new islands, they had

LOSING SCALES AND TAILS

Geckos have evolved a way to escape from predators. When a bird or other predator grabs the gecko's tail, the tail breaks off and later regrows. Scientists thought that this might be triggered when a panicked gecko released a chemical that would cause tissue in the tail to deteriorate. Scientists used a variety of microscopes to study the structure of geckos' tails. They saw a zigzagged line in each tail and realized it was along this line that the tails broke off. Scientists discovered that the tail does not separate because of a chemical. Instead, special surfaces on the tail side and the body side allow the tail to stay in place unless it is tugged.

A newly discovered species of gecko, *Geckolepis megalepis*, has large body scales that, like the tails of other geckos, have a tear zone. This breaking point makes it easy for these geckos to quickly shed scales when grabbed. Scientists believe that, as with the shedding of tails, the shedding of scales helps them escape predators.

nowhere else to go in search of food. The first thing that happened was that the largest species of lizards died off. There simply wasn't enough prey available to provide the food needed for these larger animals to survive. The death of the larger lizards left the *Gymnodactylus amarali*, a dragonfly-sized gecko, as the principal predator of the termites.

The heads of some members of the gecko population were too small to be able to eat the termites. Like the largest lizard species, the small-headed geckos died off. The geckos that had slightly larger heads ate the termites and thrived, taking over the ecosystem. In 2011, an international team of scientists studied the gecko populations on five of these islands. They found that the geckos there had larger heads than those at five nearby mainland sites that they also studied. The researchers also noted that both male and female geckos had larger heads, so the trait isn't simply an example of sexual dimorphism.

Some scientists believe that the change was simply due to improved nutrition. Without the presence of larger predators, the geckos on the islands had less competition for prey than did the geckos on the mainland. But the scientists involved believe that they are seeing adaptation and evolution to a change in the geckos' environment. The evidence comes not only from the changes in the geckos themselves but in rapid evolution seen in other reptiles such as the green anoles living in Florida. In the late 1990s, brown anoles from Cuba made their way onto Florida

Geckos can climb on walls and even ceilings in people's homes.

islands where green anoles, *A. carolinensis*, already lived. Scientists watched to see what would happen, because the lizards are similar in size and eat the same things. Green anoles moved higher up in the trees. In only 15 years, green anoles had evolved broader toe pads to help them stick as they climbed. Scientists have learned that a change in the competition for resources or a change in the resources available, as well as isolation, can fuel rapid evolution in reptiles.

CHAPTER SEVEN

Monitor Lizards

The 80 species of monitor lizards are fairly easy to recognize.[1] As a group, they are long and low to the ground with muscular bodies, elongated heads, and powerful legs. They live throughout sub-Saharan Africa, southern and Southeast Asia, Australia, and the Pacific Islands. Smaller species grow to only eight inches (20 cm) long, but the largest monitor is also the most well known. Indonesia's Komodo dragon, which gets its name from one of the islands it lives on, can reach ten feet (3 m) long, although it is not the only large monitor. The water monitor of Southeast Asia can grow to nine feet (2.7 m) long.[2] Monitor lizards have clawed feet, and all but the largest

Komodo dragons sometimes fight each other to determine dominance.

are excellent climbers. Unlike most reptiles, monitors grow their entire lives, so the largest lizards within any population are also the oldest.

Different from many lizards, monitors have a bifurcated tongue. This means that, like a snake's tongue, their tongue is split at the tip. Also like a snake, the monitor flicks its tongue out to pick up chemical scents. It then pulls its tongue back into its mouth, where a special scent organ on the roof of its mouth analyzes the chemicals.

VARANUS OBOR

In places from rain forests to small islands, new animals are still being discovered by science. The torch monitor, or *Varanus obor*, was spotted in 2009 on the Indonesian island of Sanana by Valter Weijola, a graduate student at Åbo Akademi University in Turku, Finland. The lizard got its common name because it has a black body and an orange head. This monitor can grow to a length of nearly four feet (1.2 m) and feeds on small animals and carrion in coastal sago palm swamps.[3] In Indonesia, there are no large mammalian predators. That ecosystem role is filled by monitor lizards.

Most monitors are carnivorous, with two exceptions: the Sierra Madre forest monitor and Gray's monitor. The Sierra Madre forest monitor eats primarily fruit. Gray's monitor is omnivorous, eating both prey and fruit. The omnivorous Gray's monitor was believed to be extinct until the 1980s, when a small population was found on several islands in the Philippines.

Other monitor lizards eat a variety of prey depending on the lizard's size. Prey includes

insects and spiders, lizards, small mammals, and birds. Komodo dragons capture much larger prey, including water buffalo. Monitors are active hunters, stalking their prey during the day. They also eat carrion, or dead animals, and eggs.

When threatened, monitors can deliver a painful bite, and the largest can even kill a person. In addition to a powerful bite, they whip their long tails, using them as weapons. They also swim well, and most will take to the water to avoid predators. Once in the water, they can submerge and walk across the bottom.

ORIGIN STORY

Little is known about the evolution of monitors because of the scarcity of fossils. Not only are

DRAGON VENOM

The force of a Komodo dragon's bite is enough to kill most prey, but it also has venom glands in its lower jaws. In 2009, a group of scientists described the series of ducts between the lizard's teeth that allow the venom to seep into the saliva and from there to the wound. Toxins found in this venom can cause prey to go into shock. The toxins also prevent the blood from clotting, so the animal will bleed heavily. Some scientists believe that the venom was essential to kill prey earlier in the reptile's evolutionary history, but now that the Komodo dragon has such a vicious bite, the venom is simply a remnant. But other scientists who have studied the lizard's venom delivery system disagree. They point out that other lizards and snakes that no longer need venom lose the ability to produce such toxins. Further research is needed to determine how the toxins continue to help the Komodo dragon.

there few specimens but most consist only of a handful of vertebrae. With only a fraction of a skeleton, it is easy to misidentify a set of remains. Yet scientists are still looking for answers.

There have been three main theories regarding the origin and migration of monitor lizards. The first is that these lizards originated in Asia and then moved into Africa and Australia. The second has the lizards originating in Africa before dispersing into Asia and Australia. In the final theory, monitors originated in Gondwana prior to any of the major plate movements.

In 2012, a group of scientists published the results of a molecular study in the journal *Biology Letters*. To discover where and when monitors diversified, the team had created a molecular database for 54 species of anguimorph lizards.[4] This group includes the monitors and their relatives the gila monsters.

ANCIENT AFRICAN FOSSIL

In 2010, scientists from the University of Alberta examined the fossil of a 33-million-year-old lizard. The vertebrae of this fossil closely resemble those of the modern Komodo dragon. They believe that this similarity and the age of the fossil indicate it is an ancestor to modern Komodo dragons. They also believe monitors originated in Africa, where the fossil was found. Although many modern monitors are adequate swimmers, the distance from Africa to Indonesia would be too great for the lizard to swim. Some scientists believe that plate tectonics shifted small landmasses, allowing monitors and other animals to migrate plate by plate across the globe. Others think monitors traveled overland through the Middle East.

The group focused its study on several specific gene groupings. One group of genes affected proteins, and the other group of genes affected bone. Comparing these genes, the scientists were able to determine not only when monitors diversified as a group but also when they migrated to various areas. According to the molecular data, monitors originated in Asia approximately 82 MYA. They then spread into Africa from 49 to 33 MYA. This finding is supported by the fact that there are no monitors in Madagascar, an island that separated from the African mainland 160 to 117 MYA. Monitors then moved into Australia from 39 to 26 MYA, around the same time that pythons, blind snakes, and other lizards are thought to have migrated into this area.

THE FIRST GIANT

Another group of scientists, which published its results in 2012, came to a different conclusion. Its findings came from fossils found decades earlier. Between 1921 and 1924, Barnum Brown excavated a fossil from a site in Samos, Greece, known as Quarry 1. Identified as part of a group of fossilized mammal bones, it was added to the collection of New York's American Museum of Natural History. In 2009, Dr. Nikos Solounias, an expert in evolutionary biology, recognized that the bones were reptilian. He told Carl Mehling of the museum's Department of Paleontology.

Water monitors are
excellent swimmers.

Like other monitor fossils, this fossil was incomplete, consisting of the right side of the

braincase, part of the lower jaw, fragments of a clavicle (or collarbone), and parts of six

vertebrae. From this, Mehling and other researchers recognized the remains of a monitor.

Computer modeling and comparisons with living monitors enabled them to estimate the size

of this lizard at 2 to 2.6 feet (0.6–0.8 m) long. It is longer than 99 percent of lizards past and

present.[5]

They named this monitor the Samos dragon, *Varanus amnhophilis*. It is the oldest giant

monitor lizard found to date. This discovery is especially significant because most large monitors

evolve where no large mammalian predators live. But the Samos dragon evolved alongside mammalian competition. Some of these mammals were mustelids, which include modern weasels and badgers; hyaenids, which include modern hyenas; and suids, which include modern boars.

SUPER SIZED

At one time, scientists thought that the Komodo dragon evolved to its large size after it reached its current range in Indonesia. That theory was disproved in 2009. Scott Hocknull of the Queensland Museum, Australia, along with other researchers from Indonesia and Malaysia, surveyed the fossil record. They found that over the course of four million years, large monitors had lived in India, Indonesia, and Australia. The largest, Megalania, known scientifically as *Varanus priscus*, was 16.4 feet (5 m) long.[6] It lived in Australia until it died out 40,000 years ago.

Australian fossils excavated from 2006 to 2009 show that Megalania and the Komodo dragon lived in Australia at the same time.

ESTIMATING SIZE

When scientists have only a partial skeleton, they have to estimate the total size of the animal. For *Varanus amnhophilis*, they had the braincase, lower jaw, vertebrae, and a pelvis fragment. To figure out how long this animal was, they looked at the braincase and corresponding vertebrae of 20 modern skeletons from 15 different species of monitor lizards.[7] Computer analysis of the measurements of modern skeletons allowed them to come up with an estimate for *V. amnhophilis*.

"We've unearthed numerous fossils from eastern Australia dated from 300,000 years ago to approximately four million years ago that we now know to be the Komodo dragon," said Hocknull. "When we compared these fossils to the bones of present-day Komodo dragons, they were identical."[8]

These finds indicated that the Komodo dragon actually evolved in Australia around 3.8 MYA. Some of these giant lizards remained in Australia until 130,000 years ago. Others island-hopped, swimming from island to island until they reached Timor, Flores, and Java in Indonesia. They only survived on Java briefly. But they have been on Flores for approximately 900,000 years. Hocknull hopes that understanding the evolution and migration of the Komodo dragon will help save the world's largest living lizard from extinction.

Megalania is the largest known lizard to have lived on land.

CHAPTER EIGHT

Chameleons

Chameleons live in Africa, the Middle East, and countries around the Indian Ocean. All of the more than 200 species of these lizards can change color.[1] Originally, people thought chameleons changed color to match their background as a form of camouflage. In cartoons, chameleons were shown doing things like changing to match a polka-dot background and changing again when the background switched to stripes. But chameleons don't pay attention to the background when they change. Each species has a range of colors and patterns that they display to communicate with each other.

Chameleons change color for a variety of reasons. The more dominant a male chameleon is, the brighter his colors. This helps him tell other males to stay out of his territory. A male that gets defeated in a struggle over territory and wants to look submissive will become

Panther chameleons are some of the most colorful chameleons.

more brown or gray. A female chameleon that is approached by a male may adopt a color pattern that tells him to go away because she is already pregnant.

The top layer of a chameleon's skin is the epidermis, the protective outer layer all animals have. In chameleons, the next three layers of skin control their colors. The layer below the epidermis, the chromatophore layer, contains red and yellow pigments. Beneath this, the melanophore layer has melanin, the dark pigment used to create browns and black and to reflect blue. The nether layer reflects white. Nerve impulses and hormone changes alter the color cells, causing them to expand and shrink to create a wide variety of color patterns.

Chameleons can also be recognized by their protruding eyes. Each eye is covered by a cone-shaped eyelid. A chameleon can move and focus its eyes independently. This means it can look at two different things at the same time and can see all the way around its body with no blind spots.

SPECIES OR NOT?

When someone spots what may be a new plant or animal, one of the first tasks that scientists undertake is to decide whether it is a new species. That's what scientists did in 2012 when they found four tiny chameleons on Madagascar. It isn't enough that an animal looks different, because a male animal can look different from a female. Juveniles often look different as well. The scientists had to show that each of the four came from a population of chameleons distinct from other populations. They did this by sampling the animals' DNA and constructing a family tree.

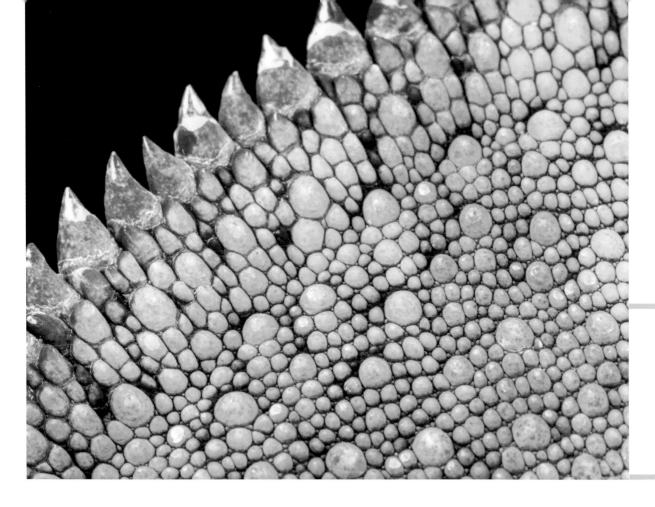

Chameleons can create different color patterns on their bodies.

Most chameleons eat insects, but the largest may also eat lizards and birds. When a chameleon spots a potential meal, both eyes focus on its prey. The chameleon has a long tongue, which it flicks at the prey animal. When it hits, the ball of muscle on the tongue's tip forms a suction cup and sticks to the prey. The chameleon pulls the animal in and crunches it up. Chameleons move very slowly, but their tongues enable them to catch fast-moving prey.

CRETACEOUS DIVERSIFICATION

Most lizard families diversified during the Jurassic period (201.3 to 145 MYA), but chameleons diversified late in the Cretaceous. Part of the reason for this is probably due to climate and the spread of forests. During the Cretaceous, tropical forest and open-canopy forest had spread through Africa and Madagascar, giving the chameleon new, open niches to exploit. The chameleon had already evolved its opposable digits, rotating eyes (pictured), and tongue. These would have been ideal for hunting in open forest, a new niche chameleons moved into.

CHAMELEON GENES

In 2013, Krystal Tolley of the Department of Botany and Zoology of the University of Stellenbosch, South Africa, and two fellow researchers published a paper on chameleon origins. The goal of their study was to find out when these lizards diversified. The three scientists studied between six and 13 genetic markers in more than 90 percent of the known species of chameleons.[2]

What they found was that chameleons had split from their next-closest reptile relative in the middle to late part of the Cretaceous. The six chameleon genera had divided in the mid part of the Paleogene period (66–23 MYA). Individual species differentiated mainly during the late part of the Paleogene.

Tolley and the others believe that chameleons initially lived in forest environments with large perches and slender tree branches. Only more recently, when species diversified to a wider variety of niches, did they spread into habitats with small perches, including grasses, small bushes, and mountainous plants. As new environments became available during the late part of the Paleogene, they created new opportunities for this group of lizards.

Their research shows three migrations out of Africa. Approximately 65 MYA and then again 47 MYA, chameleons migrated from Africa to Madagascar. The third species movement occurred approximately 34 MYA when chameleons moved from Africa to the Indian Ocean's Seychelles islands. This means that

EXPLOSION AND DECLINE

Adaptive radiation is a phenomenon that occurs when one species evolves into a number of new species. This happens when animals move into niches in which they have little or no competition, such as an island with no other predators or a new grassland in which the animal is perfectly camouflaged. Any empty niche is an opportunity for a life-form poised to take advantage of it. Specialization also leads to radiation. Animals might develop a mutation that minimizes competition, such as the ability to feed on a new food or more easily capture food. When an animal is capable of feeding on something that no other animal eats, it is likely to adapt in ways that allow it to take advantage of this niche. All of these factors can lead to rapid diversification. When a niche is filled with species or there is a radical environmental change, competition increases and some of these animals will die off.

Chameleon tongues help them catch their food.

chameleons crossed open water on rafts of vegetation carried by ocean currents, which took them from one landmass to another.

CHAMELEON IN AMBER

When scientists examined the amber from Burma that contained 12 fossilized lizards, they not only found a gecko but also a chameleon. Because the amber dated to 100 MYA, this was the oldest fossilized chameleon ever found. Eighty million years older than the next-oldest chameleon fossil, it challenges the idea that chameleons evolved in Africa.

Edward Stanley, a University of Florida postdoctoral student in herpetology at the Florida Museum of Natural History, used technology to learn more about these lizards. "It was mind-blowing," he said about examining the fossils. "Usually we have a foot or other small part preserved in amber, but these are whole specimens—claws, toepads, teeth, even perfectly intact colored scales. I was familiar with CT technology, so I realized this was an opportunity to look more closely and put the lizards into evolutionary perspective."[3]

Although the lizard doesn't have all of the trademark features, Stanley realized that the animal he was seeing in the scans was a chameleon. The dime-sized fossil doesn't have the fused toes ending in claws that enable modern chameleons to hang onto branches. But it does have the large bone that anchors the chameleon's long, sticky tongue. This gives scientists some idea of the order in which the chameleon's unique features evolved.

Stanley also feels that finding such a wide range of lizards in one area stresses the need for conservation. "These exquisitely preserved examples of past diversity show us why we should be protecting these areas where their modern relatives live today," Stanley said. "The tropics often act as a stable refuge where biodiversity tends to accumulate, while other places are more variable in terms of climate and species. However, the tropics are not impervious to human efforts to destroy them."[4]

RATE DECLINES

Although Madagascar contains only 1 percent of the world's land, it is home to approximately 3 percent of Earth's species.[5] Daniel Scantlebury, who was a biology PhD student at the University of Rochester, New York, studied several chameleon species as part of his degree to see whether the level of diversity in Madagascar was holding steady or in a decline.

"A staggering number of species are found only on Madagascar," said Scantlebury. "But this research shows there are limits to the number of species the island can sustain and Madagascar may currently be at those limits." To measure the rates of diversity in the past, Scantlebury analyzed the evolutionary records of seven groups of Madagascar's reptiles and amphibians, including leaf chameleons and day geckos. He created an evolutionary tree to compare the ages of the species studied.[6]

He found that since 90 MYA, when Madagascar separated from the African continent, the speed at which new species develop has slowed. Species diversify rapidly when an environment, such as an island, has many unexploited niches. As niches are filled and the competition increases, a habitat reaches the point that it cannot support any additional species, causing diversification to slow or stop.

Many chameleon species in the genus *Furcifer* live only in Madagascar.

Scantlebury hopes that his work will encourage other scientists to conduct similar studies. "I am curious to know if this pattern holds for other iconic groups of Madagascan species, such as lemurs and crown-of-thorn plants," he says.[7] Only then will scientists know whether this decline is taking place throughout Madagascar or even across the planet.

Like geckos, anoles are excellent climbers.

CHAPTER NINE

New Discoveries

Between the scanty fossil record and the fact that various findings contradict each other, it is clear that there is still much to learn about the evolution of reptiles. New technologies and new theories will make a big impact. Often, it is students who are leading the way. One of these students, graduate student Shane Campbell-Staton, wanted to learn how cold affected anoles.

The idea that extreme weather could contribute to the evolution of a species is not new. In 1898, naturalist Hermon Bumpus of Brown University sampled house sparrows that had died in a blizzard. He observed that larger males were more likely than smaller males to survive extreme winter weather and to reproduce. Medium-sized

ANOLES

More than 400 species of anoles live throughout the Americas.[2] These small tree-dwelling lizards are close kin to iguanas. Like geckos, many anoles have enlarged toe pads. Unlike the toe pads of geckos, which are covered in microscopic fibers, anoles' toe pads are covered with tiny hooks that allow them to climb up walls and tree trunks. Anoles are sexually dimorphic, with the males having a dewlap, or throat fan. These dewlaps are often brightly colored. When a male extends its dewlap, the color signals to other males that he is in possession of a given territory and tells females that he is available for mating.

females were more likely to survive. More recently, scientists have observed changes in Brazilian geckos living on newly created islands.

Campbell-Staton wanted to know how anoles adapted to cold weather. Although their ancestors came from Cuba, the lizards now live across the southeastern United States in areas cooler than their homeland. Campbell-Staton spent several years studying anoles from five different latitudes. He wanted to find out at what temperature they ceased to function. He tested this by putting anoles into a chamber he could slowly cool. When researchers flip an anole onto its back, it turns itself back over if it is functioning well. If it lacks the coordination to do this, it is too cold. Campbell-Staton found that lizards near the southern end of the range lost function at 52 degrees Fahrenheit (11°C). Lizards at the northern edge of the range functioned in temperatures as low as 42.8 degrees Fahrenheit (6°C).[1]

In the winter of 2013 to 2014, a polar vortex caused Texas's lowest temperatures in 15 years. In northern Texas, the cold lasted only a week, but in Brownsville in the south, it lasted for a month. Normally when a weather event such as this occurs, scientists have no data from before the event to use as a comparison. Campbell-Staton not only had that information, he took advantage of the opportunity to learn even more.

In the spring, Campbell-Staton collected more data on the anoles. The surviving Brownsville anoles now had the same cold tolerance as the northernmost anoles. Not only could they function at colder temperatures, but when Campbell-Staton examined their livers, he found active genes that had not been

MARY ANNING

Today, students are pushing the study of ancient life forward. But perhaps the youngest and most prolific fossil hunter ever was Mary Anning. Anning was born in 1799 in Lyme Regis, England. In 1811, when her brother found what he thought was a crocodile skull, he gave Mary the job of digging it up. Twelve-year-old Mary recovered not only the skull but also 60 vertebrae of what turned out to be an ichthyosaurus, an ancient marine reptile.[3] Mary never went to college and had very little formal education. She taught herself paleontology, geology, anatomy, and how to draw scientific illustrations. She went on to become one of the most accomplished fossil hunters, finding more ichthyosaurs, another marine reptile called a plesiosaur, and many other fossils. Until recently, it was the scientists to whom she sold her fossils who got the credit for her finds. The Natural History Museum in London has made Anning and her finds a core attraction in its Fossil Marine Reptiles Gallery.

active before the vortex. The active genes in their livers now resembled those of northern Texas anoles. These included genes that control the function of the nervous and muscular systems, systems that would improve their coordination at lower temperatures.

"The temptation from results like these is to assume extreme events drive much of evolutionary change, but it may not be that simple," says Butch Brodie, director of the University of Virginia Mountain Lake Biological Station in Pembroke.[4] He reminds people that the anoles' cold tolerance may be temporary. An anomaly may cause a change in a species, but without the pressure to continue selecting for a trait, its adaptation may disappear. In addition, Brodie emphasized that a change that enables cold tolerance could mean that the anoles function less well in warmer temperatures.

NEW FOSSILS

In 2012, the fossils of six young adult dinosaurs were found in a quarry in southern Argentina. Scientists named this new species *Patagotitan mayorum*. Diego Pol of the Egidio Feruglio paleontology museum in Argentina coauthored the study, printed in the journal *Proceedings of the Royal Society B*, in 2017. The study revealed the dinosaurs lived 100 MYA based on the date of the ash that lay around the fossils.

A cast of the *Patagotitan mayorum* fossil went on display at the Field Museum in Chicago, Illinois, in 2018.

It took scientists more than a year to excavate the *P. mayorum* fossils including vertebrae, hind leg and foreleg bones, ribs, and part of a hip. From these bones, the paleontologists estimate that this dinosaur weighed 76 tons (69 metric tons) and was 122 feet (37 m) long and nearly 20 feet (6 m) tall at the shoulder.[5] *Patagotitan mayorum* may have been the largest land animal that ever lived. This sauropod had a long neck that helped it reach leaves.

But size isn't the only reason the find is important. "For the first time, we have the opportunity to assess how these giants were built, what adaptations they had in their anatomy, how they could cope with such a massive weight," Pol says.[6] Scientists believe these dinosaurs grew so big because food was readily available in the forests and flowering plants grew widely at this time.

Scientists continue to search for reptile fossils.

Before scientists can study a fossil, it has to be discovered. Sometimes a find is made by quarry workers. Rich McCrea, curator of the Canadian Museum of Nature in Ottawa, Ontario, says anyone can find a fossil, although young people are especially good at it. They pay close attention to what they see because they believe that they can find something spectacular. When they spot something, they are more likely to believe that they've found a fossil. When adults see the same thing, they may convince themselves that they haven't found anything special.

NEW INTERPRETATIONS

New fossils will make their way to museums, but old fossils will also be reinterpreted or reexamined after sitting on a shelf for years. In 2010, this happened with a fossil in the collection of the University of Texas at Austin. The Work Projects Administration (WPA) had found it in 1940 near Big Spring, Texas. The WPA, a work program during the Great Depression (1929–1939), focused on keeping people employed. Some of the WPA's workers were fossil hunters. Many fossils were found and collected but are still waiting to be cleaned and studied. Since its discovery, one particular fossil had been sitting in a lab at the university.

In 2010, when the skull was finally cleaned for study, Michelle Stocker, now a research scientist at Virginia Tech, was a PhD student. Sterling Nesbitt, an assistant professor of paleontology at Virginia Tech, was a postdoctoral researcher. They published a paper identifying the skull in 2016 in the journal *Current Biology*. They identified the fossil as a previously unknown reptile they named *Triopticus primus*. It had a thick, dome-shaped skull with a large pit on top that looked like a third eye. The creature's name means "the first with three eyes." It lived more than 200 MYA.

"After the enormous mass extinction 250 million years ago, reptiles exploded onto the scene and almost immediately diversified into many different sizes and shapes. These early body shapes were later mimicked by dinosaurs," said Nesbitt.[7] One of these shapes is the dome-shaped head of *T. primus*. The repetition in body shapes from earlier reptiles to later

ULTRACONSERVED ELEMENTS

UCEs don't exist only between turtles, lizards, dinosaurs, and snakes. They also exist between human beings and birds. Although common ancestors eventually evolved into very distantly related species, these modern species still share similar sections of genome. Because UCEs have remained consistent through extremely different life-forms, scientists know that they must have a function. However, when scientists made these segments inoperative in mice, the offspring could still survive and reproduce. Still, mutations in these segments have not occurred, which leads scientists to believe that they function in some way that remains a mystery.

dinosaurs makes scientists like Stocker and Nesbitt wonder what forces acted on both groups of animals to lead to similar body types.

NEW DATA

New data will also play a part in scientists' learning more about the evolution of reptiles. In 2014, ultraconserved elements (UCEs) helped scientists create a new family tree for turtles. UCEs are segments of genomes that are very similar across many species. The technique has been available since 2012, but scientists are only now beginning to take advantage of what it can reveal.

A team of scientists, including researchers from the California Academy of Sciences, compared UCEs from many species. The authors created a new taxonomic group with the information they collected. This group is Archelosauria, and it includes turtles, birds, crocodiles, and dinosaurs. Turtles are more distantly related to the other reptiles.

One of the authors, James Parham, is an assistant professor of geological sciences at Cal State Fullerton and widely acknowledged as an expert on turtles. "I have been working on the evolutionary relationships of turtles for over 20 years using a variety of methods," says Parham. "Fossils are essential for showing us what extinct turtles looked like, but also in letting us know when and where they lived in the past."[8]

But fossils alone don't yield an accurate picture of the turtle's evolution. "These new testing techniques help reconcile the information from DNA and fossils, making us confident that we've found the right tree," says Parham.[9] As more DNA is compiled and new techniques come into play, more information on reptiles past and present will become available. This, paired with growing knowledge of the fossil record, will yield an increasingly accurate picture of the evolution of all reptiles.

PERIOD TIMELINE						Hylonomus lyelli	Eunotosaurus	
	541–485.4 million years ago (MYA)	485.4–443.8 MYA	443.8–419.2 MYA	419.2–358.9 MYA	358.9–298.9 MYA	298.9–251.9 MYA	
	CAMBRIAN	ORDOVICIAN	SILURIAN	DEVONIAN	CARBONIFEROUS	PERMIAN	

NUMBER OF SPECIES

There are more than 10,000 species of reptiles according to the Reptile Database maintained by Peter Uetz at the Center for the Study of Biological Complexity at Virginia Commonwealth University.

IMPORTANT ANIMALS AND SPECIMENS

- The oldest reptile fossil is *Hylonomus lyelli*, which lived about 350 MYA and looked like a lizard.

- Australia's tuatara looks like a lizard but is the only living rhynchocephalian.

- The oldest turtle, *Eunotosaurus*, had no shell and lived 260 MYA in South Africa. Its broad ribs provided muscle attachments that helped it dig. Broad ribs later evolved into a protective shell.

- Snakes evolved from fossorial, or burrowing, lizards.

- The oldest fossil chameleon and fossil gecko both lived 100 MYA and were fossilized in amber in Burma.

TRIASSIC	JURASSIC	CRETACEOUS	PALEOGENE	NEOGENE	QUATERNARY
Carnufex		oldest fossil chameleon and fossil gecko *Mansourasaurus shahinae*			tuatara
251.9–201.3 MYA	201.3–145 MYA	145–66 MYA	66–23 MYA	23–2.6 MYA	2.6 MYA–present

IMPORTANT SCIENTISTS

○ Dr. Hesham Sallam, head of the Department of Geology at Mansoura University in Mansoura, Egypt, was part of the team that discovered *Mansourasaurus shahinae* in 2013.

○ Huanming Yang at Beijing Genomics Institute and Xiaosong Gu at Nantong University sequenced the first gecko genome in 2015. At the time, this was the largest reptile genome that had ever been sequenced.

○ David Lambert from New Zealand's Massey University and his fellow researchers published an article on tuatara genetics in the journal *Trends in Genetics* in March 2008. The group is studying the rate, or speed, at which tuatara are evolving.

QUOTE

"These new testing techniques help reconcile the information from DNA and fossils, making us confident that we've found the right tree."

—James Parham, assistant professor of geological sciences at California State University, Fullerton, speaking about turtles in 2014

GLOSSARY

adaptation
A change in traits within a population that is caused by different conditions in the environment.

carapace
The hard upper shell of a turtle, tortoise, or terrapin.

climate change
A process affecting the planet that is causing temperatures around the world to rise.

crustacean
A typically aquatic invertebrate with an exoskeleton and two pairs of antennae; includes crabs, barnacles, and shrimp.

CT scanner
A machine that uses CT scanning technology, also called high-resolution X-ray tomography, an imaging process that results in a three-dimensional image.

diverge
To split into two or more species.

diversify
To multiply in such a way that some individuals have different traits than others.

DNA
Deoxyribonucleic acid, the chemical that is the basis of genetics, through which various traits are passed from parent to child.

excavate
To dig up.

gene
A unit of hereditary information found in a chromosome.

genome
An organism's genetic material.

greenhouse gas

A gas that absorbs infrared radiation and traps heat in the atmosphere.

herpetologist

Someone who studies reptiles and amphibians.

invasive

Describing an organism that arrives in a new ecosystem, takes over, and causes harm.

juvenile

A young individual who is not yet fully mature.

molecular

Having to do with molecules, the smallest unit into which a substance can be broken down that is made of two or more atoms and has all of the same properties of the original substance.

parietal eye

An eyelike structure on top of the head.

trait

A genetically determined and environmentally shaped characteristic.

SELECTED BIBLIOGRAPHY

Chambers, Delaney. "Why Snakes Don't Have Legs (for Now)." *National Geographic*, 23 Oct. 2016, nationalgeographic.com.au. Accessed 30 Mar. 2018.

Lillywhite, Harvey B. *How Snakes Work: Structure, Function, and Behavior of the World's Snakes*. Oxford UP, 2014.

Tolley, Krystal A., and Anthony Herrell. *The Biology of Chameleons*. U of California, 2013.

FURTHER READINGS

Dinosaurs: A Visual Encyclopedia. 2nd ed., DK, 2018.

McCarthy, Colin. *Reptile*. 3rd American ed., DK, 2017.

Zug, George R., and Carl H. Ernst. *Snakes in Question*. 2nd ed., Smithsonian Institution, 2015.

ONLINE RESOURCES

Booklinks
NONFICTION NETWORK
FREE! ONLINE NONFICTION RESOURCES

To learn more about the evolution of reptiles, visit **abdobooklinks.com**. These links are routinely monitored and updated to provide the most current information available.

MORE INFORMATION

For more information on this subject, contact or visit the following organizations:

THE AMERICAN MUSEUM OF NATURAL HISTORY
Central Park W. at Seventy-Ninth Street
New York, NY 10024-5192
212-769-5100
amnh.org

The Hall of Amphibians and Reptiles explores the anatomy, defenses, locomotion, distribution, and food habits of these animals.

THE FIELD MUSEUM
1400 S. Lake Shore Drive
Chicago, IL 60605-2496
312-922-9410
fieldmuseum.org

The collections at this museum include fossils and dinosaurs, as well as information on living species.

SOURCE NOTES

CHAPTER 1. THE END OF THE AGE OF THE DINOSAURS

1. Karen Kaplan. "This Dinosaur from Egypt Is a Really Big Deal—In More Ways than One." *Los Angeles Times*, 29 Jan. 2018, latimes.com. Accessed 10 Aug. 2018.

2. "Rare Dinosaur Discovery in Egypt Could Signal More Finds." *VOA*, 7 Feb. 2018, voanews.com. Accessed 10 Aug. 2018.

3. "A New Dinosaur Species Named 'Mansourasaurus Shahinae' Discovered in Egypt." *YouTube*, uploaded by Hindustan Times, 11 Feb. 2018, youtube.com. Accessed 10 Aug. 2018.

4. Sathya Achia Abraham. "Reptile Database Surpasses 10,000 Reptile Species." *Phys.org*, 1 Aug. 2014, phys.org. Accessed 10 Aug. 2018.

5. "Hylonomus: The Earliest Reptile." *Canadian Museum of Nature*, 3 Mar. 2017, nature.ca. Accessed 10 Aug. 2018.

CHAPTER 2. TUATARA

1. Natalie Angier. "Reptiles Pet-Store Looks Belie Its Triassic Appeal." *New York Times*, 22 Nov. 2010, nytimes.com. Accessed 10 Aug. 2018.

2. "Tuatara." *Department of Conservation Te Papa Atawhai*, n.d., doc.govt.nz. Accessed 10 Aug. 2018.

3. "Tuatara: *Sphenodon punctatus*." *San Diego Zoo*, 2018, animals.sandiegozoo.org. Accessed 10 Aug. 2018.

4. G. Y. Walls. "Activity of the Tuatara and Its Relationships to Weather Conditions on Stephens Island, Cook Strait, with Observations on Geckos and Invertebrates." *New Zealand Journal of Zoology*, vol. 10, no. 3, 16 Jan. 2012, pp. 309–317, tandfonline.com. Accessed 10 Aug. 2018.

5. Heidi Ledford. "The Rapid Evolution of Tuatara." *Nature*, 27 Mar. 2008, nature.com. Accessed 10 Aug. 2018.

6. Ledford, "The Rapid Evolution of Tuatara."

7. Ledford, "The Rapid Evolution of Tuatara."

CHAPTER 3. TURTLES

1. Ed Yong. "Why Turtles Evolved Shells: It Wasn't for Protection." *Atlantic*, 14 July 2016, theatlantic.com. Accessed 10 Aug. 2018.

2. "Desmatochelys padillai: Paleontologists Find Oldest Known Species of Sea Turtle." *Sci-News*, 7 Sept. 2015, sci-news.com. Accessed 10 Aug. 2018.

3. "Box Turtles and People." *Missouri Department of Conservation*, 29 Nov. 2010, mdc.mo.gov. Accessed 10 Aug. 2018.

4. "DNA Sequences Reveal the True Identity of the Softshell Turtle Pelodiscus." *ScienceDaily*, 5 Oct. 2011, sciencedaily.com. Accessed 10 Aug. 2018.

5. Alina Bradford. "Turtle Facts." *Live Science*, 1 Oct. 2015, livescience.com. Accessed 10 Aug. 2018.

6. C. Kenneth Dodd Jr. *North American Box Turtles: A Natural History*. U of Oklahoma P, 2001. 47.

CHAPTER 4. CROCODILIANS

1. James P. Ross and Heinz Fritz Wermuth. "Crocodile." *Encyclopædia Britannica*, 2018, britannica.com. Accessed 10 Aug. 2018.

2. "Cuvier's Smooth-Fronted Caiman." *Toronto Zoo*, n.d., torontozoo.com. Accessed 10 Aug. 2018.

3. Ross and Wermuth, "Crocodile."

4. "Nile Crocodile." *National Geographic*, 2015, nationalgeographic.com. Accessed 10 Aug. 2018.

5. "Nile Crocodile."

6. "Gharial." *National Geographic*, 2015, nationalgeographic.com. Accessed 10 Aug. 2018.

7. "American Alligator." *National Geographic*, 2015, nationalgeographic.com. Accessed 10 Aug. 2018.

8. "Caiman." *Encyclopædia Britannica*, 9 Feb. 2018, britannica.com. Accessed 10 Aug. 2018.

9. Bob Straus. "Prehistoric Crocodile: Profiles and Pictures." *ThoughtCo*, 20 Mar. 2017, thoughtco.com. Accessed 10 Aug. 2018.

10. Matthew Lindsay. "Every Fossil Tells a Story." *George Washington University*, Dec. 2004, www2.gwu.edu. Accessed 10 Aug. 2018.

11. Tim Stephens. "Scientists Reconstruct Genome of Common Ancestor of Crocodiles, Birds, Dinosaurs." *UC Santa Cruz News Center*, 11 Dec. 2014, news.ucsc.edu. Accessed 10 Aug. 2018.

12. Stephens, "Scientists Reconstruct Genome of Common Ancestor."

13. Stephens, "Scientists Reconstruct Genome of Common Ancestor."

CHAPTER 5. SNAKES

1. "Lizard Classification: Ornate Sandveld Lizard." *Siyabona Africa*, 2017, krugerpark.co.za. Accessed 20 Aug. 2018.

2. Agata Blaszczak-Boxe. "Oldest Known Snake Fossils Identified." *Live Science*, 27 Jan. 2015, livescience.com. Accessed 10 Aug. 2018.

3. "Mosasaur Fossils." *Alabama Museum of Natural History*, n.d., almnh.ua.edu. Accessed 10 Aug. 2018.

4. University of Helsinki. "The Origin of Snakes: New Evolutionary Scenario." *Science News*, 25 Jan. 2018, sciencedaily.com. Accessed 10 Aug. 2018.

5. Sathya Achia Abraham. "Toxic Snake Venom to Fight Human Disease." *VCU News*, 27 Sept. 2006, news.vcu.edu. Accessed 20 Aug. 2018.

6. Oishimaya Sen Nag. "How Many Types of Cobras Are There? Which Species Are Most Venomous?" *WorldAtlas*, 31 May 2018. Accessed 10 Aug. 2018.

7. Email correspondence with Peter Uetz, 20 Aug. 2018.

CHAPTER 6. GECKOS

1. Juan D. Daza et al. "Mid-Cretaceous Amber Fossils Illuminate the Past Diversity of Tropical Lizards." *Science Advances*, vol. 2, no. 3, Mar. 2016, researchgate.net. Accessed 17 Aug. 2018.

2. Maya Wei-Haas. "Pint-Sized Lizards Trapped in Amber Give Clues to Life 100 Million Years Ago." *Smithsonian.com*, 4 Mar. 2016, smithsonianmag.com. Accessed 17 Aug. 2018.

3. David Burnie and Don E. Wilson, editors. *Animal: The Definitive Visual Guide*. 1st American ed., DK, 2001. 417.

4. Alina Bradford. "Facts about Geckos." *LiveScience*, 25 Aug. 2017, livescience.com. 17 Aug. 2018.

5. Yan Liu et al. "*Gekko japonicus* Genome Reveals Evolution of Adhesive Toe Pads and Tail Regeneration." *Nature*, vol. 6, no. 10033, 2015, nature.com. Accessed 17 Aug. 2018.

6. Liu et al. "*Gekko japonicus* Genome."

7. "How Sticky Toepads Evolved in Geckos and What That Means for Adhesive Technologies." *Phys.org*, 27 June 2012, phys.org. Accessed 17 Aug. 2018.

8. Liu et al. "*Gekko japonicus* Genome."

9. Kelsey Kennedy. "A Dam in Brazil Has Altered the Course of Evolution." *Atlas Obscura*, 1 Aug. 2017, atlasobscura.com. Accessed 17 Aug. 2018.

CHAPTER 7. MONITOR LIZARDS

1. Email correspondence with Peter Uetz, 18 July 2018.

2. Laurie Vitt. "Monitor." *Encyclopædia Britannica*, 2 Feb. 2018, britannica.com. Accessed 17 Aug. 2018.

3. "New Monitor Lizard Discovered in Indonesia." *ScienceDaily*, 27 Apr. 2010, sciencedaily.com. Accessed 20 Aug. 2018.

4. Nicolas Vidal et al. "Molecular Evidence for an Asian Origin of Monitor Lizards Followed by Tertiary Dispersals to Africa and Australasia." *Biology Letters*, vol. 8, no. 5, July 2012, pp. 853–855, researchgate.net. Accessed 20 Aug. 2018.

5. Jack L. Conrad, Ana M. Balcarel, and Carl M. Mehling. "Earliest Example of a Giant Monitor Lizard (*Varanus*, Varanidae, Squamata)." *PLOS One*, 10 Aug. 2012, journals.plos.org. Accessed 20 Aug. 2018.

6. "Animal Species: *Megalania prisca*." *Australian Museum*, 12 Oct. 2015, australianmuseum.net.au. Accessed 20 Aug. 2018.

7. Conrad et al. "Earliest Example of a Giant Monitor Lizard."

8. "Komodo Dragons Came from Aus." *Science Alert*, 2 Oct. 2009, sciencealert.com. Accessed 20 Aug. 2018.

CHAPTER 8. CHAMELEONS

1. Henry Nicholls. "The Truth about Chameleons." *BBC*, 13 Aug. 2015, bbc.com. Accessed 23 Aug. 2018.

2. Krystal A. Tolley, Ted M. Townsend, and Miguel Vences. "Large-Scale Phylogeny of Chameleons Suggests African Origins and Eocene Diversification." *Proceedings of the Royal Society B*, 27 Mar. 2013, rspb.royalsocietypublishing.org. Accessed 20 Aug. 2018.

3. "World's Oldest Chameleon Found in Amber Fossil." *Phys.org*, 7 Mar. 2016, phys.org. Accessed 20 Aug. 2018.

4. Stephenie Livingston. "World's Oldest Chameleon Found in Amber Fossil." *University of Florida News*, 4 Mar. 2016, news.ufl.edu. Accessed 20 Aug. 2018.

5. "Research Suggests Madagascar No Longer an Evolutionary Hotspot." *University of Rochester*, 10 July 2013, rochester.edu. Accessed 20 Aug. 2018.

6. "Research Suggests Madagascar No Longer an Evolutionary Hotspot."

7. "Research Suggests Madagascar No Longer an Evolutionary Hotspot."

CHAPTER 9. NEW DISCOVERIES

1. Elizabeth Pennisi. "Cold Snap Makes Lizards Evolve in Just a Few Months." *Science*, 3 Aug. 2017, sciencemag.org. Accessed 20 Aug. 2018.

2. "Study Sheds Light on Biodiversity of Anole Lizard Family Trees." *Phys.org*, 23 Feb. 2018, phys.org. Accessed 20 Aug. 2018.

3. Sarah Zielinski. "Mary Anning: An Amazing Fossil Hunter." *Smithsonian.com*, 5 Jan. 2010, smithsonianmag.com. Accessed 20 Aug. 2018.

4. Pennisi, "Cold Snap Makes Lizards Evolve."

5. Seth Borenstein. "Patagotitan mayorum: New Study Describes the Biggest Dinosaur Ever." *Phys.org*, 9 Aug. 2017, phys.org. Accessed 20 Aug. 2018.

6. Shaena Montanari. "New Dinosaur Species Was Largest Animal Ever to Walk the Earth." *National Geographic*, 9 Aug. 2017, news.nationalgeographic.com. Accessed 20 Aug. 2018.

7. "New Species of Ancient Texas Reptile Offers Clues to the Evolution of Dinosaurs." *UT News*, 22 Sept. 2016, news.utexas.edu. Accessed 20 Aug. 2018.

8. "Scientists Solve Reptile Mysteries with Landmark Study on the Evolution of Turtles." *Phys.org*, 24 Nov. 2014, phys.org. Accessed 20 Aug. 2018.

9. "Scientists Solve Reptile Mysteries."

INDEX

Sue Bradford Edwards is a longtime fossil hound. Her home collection includes a piece of a turtle shell and a clam. She is a Missouri nonfiction author who writes about science, the social sciences, and culture. She has written and cowritten 12 other books for Abdo Publishing, including *Hidden Human Computers* with Duchess Harris, *Women in Science*, and *The Dakota Access Pipeline*.